INSPIRED BY MY
FATHER

INSPIRED BY MY FATHER

Jane Harrop

Book Guild Publishing
Sussex, England

First published in Great Britain in 2011 by
The Book Guild
Pavilion View
19 New Road
Brighton, BN1 1UF

Typesetting in Bembo by
Keyboard Services, Luton, Bedfordshire

Printed in Great Britain by
CPI Antony Rowe

A catalogue record for this book is available from
The British Library

ISBN 978 1 84624 617 3

Contents

Part One

My Father's Poems for Me

To a teenage daughter...

Now you are no longer a child
To nestle inside my arms,
Can you spare a little time only
To listen, all peaceful and calm?

It's just that I still want to love you,
It's just that I still want your love.
If I do not approve all the things that you do,
I want not to dictate from above.

I want maybe to love you,
As you would want to be loved;
At arm's length seems the right distance,
We can see, we can touch, we can move.

If you reach out, you can touch me,
If I stretch, I can reach too.
I'll be there, please God, if you need me,
Smiling and waiting for you.

I just want to know you are there, love,
Beside me, yet not too close,
So that each of us walks their own pathway,
Apart, yet not too remote.

I think I will settle for arm's length,
We can touch and our eyes can meet,
We each can always go forward,
Assured of our personal strength.

Our eyes will see different vistas,
Our steps will be varying length,
But I'll know you're there
And you'll know I'm here,
Loving you, but at arm's length.

Why do I feel so close to you?
Why do I feel so near?
Why do I see you so brightly?
Why are you always so clear?

Somehow it seems you're so close to me,
Somehow of me you're a part.
Somehow your presence wraps round me,
Somehow you've taken my heart.

You're more like a sweetheart than daughter,
You're more like a friend and a mate,
You're more like a part of my being,
You're more like a part of my fate.

It's so good to feel so close to you,
It's so good your mind works like mine,
It was good to walk on the hills with you,
It's so good to be on cloud nine.

When I die, we'll never be parted,
When I die we'll walk hand in hand,
Down the lanes we have travelled together,
Through the daffodil fields of 'our land'.

Heartsease on the window sill,
Smiling down at me,
Knowing that your caring thoughts
Are still for me.

Now you have so much to love,
I yet can claim a place,
Your shining eyes still smile for me,
Keep in your heart a place.

We've had our secrets, you and I,
And what we've had we'll keep
Close to our lives and in our hearts,
Until the day we die.

On my way back to you,
I went a long way round,
Lying and dreaming,
Listening for the coming sound
Of your presence.

The merging days went on,
The endless nights drew black,
The easy way would be to slip
Over the rim, and not come back
To you again.

Someday soon now I must go,
Leave all love behind.
But smiling I will leave you,
Leaving you my mind
To care for.

I've cufflinks of silver,
I've cufflinks of gold.
Some of them new
And some of them old.
But the ones that I use are made of a pebble,
Fashioned and varnished
With a pin in the middle.
Whenever I wear them, you are that much nearer,
And your face in my mind gets that much clearer.
As in a conch shell
You hear the sound of the sea,
So wearing your cufflinks,
Brings you closer to me.

When you said, 'What shall
I do when you are gone?'
I almost broke my heart.
Then I remembered that all is one,
Much greater than any part.
I wrote when you were a girl
That arm's length was just about right,
So if I go from earthly things
Don't worry, I'll not be far.
Don't worry about the years to come,
What we've had is ours to keep
And I'll be around when daffodils bloom.
No need for you to weep.

I love to hear the sound of your voice,
I'm happy when you are near,
And yet and yet, as the years go by,
I want to be alone.

Not alone in the lonely sense,
But turned into myself,
So that all the things that I have been
Can join with the things I've seen.

To turn the clock back to my youth
To stand and say, 'I am',
To be alone and feel complete,
To stand and feel I'm whole.

The telly makes an awful noise,
People's chatter jars.
I just want, please, to be alone
And hear the silence roar.

Part Two

My Father's Poems

Crocus colour fills the green
Close to the parish church,
Blue, yellow, mauve and white,
A patchwork of beauty seen.

The blue are sturdy, upright, strong,
Birds have pecked at the yellow,
The white are growing shyly,
The mauve are few, but belong.

It needs the pale March sunshine
To make the colours merge,
As I just wander idly
Along the roadside verge.

Is it Paradise,
The view from your window
As I lie in bed?
Passing my later years
In quietude.

Cows, with their calves
Keeping close.
Lambs skipping cleverly,
Four legs at a time.

The hill over there
Smothered in bluebells,
Ringing a spring peal
If you only listen and hear.

I lie and look,
Remembering days past,
And feel happy.
At being so close to Heaven.

Not far to go,
Between here and what
Comes after.

I think of the places I might have gone,
I think of the things I might have done.
I think of the books I should have read,
I think of the things I might have said.
I think I could have been more kind,
I think I could more love have tried.

And yet...

I think I have more friends than many.
I think I have more family love.
I feel I have more arms around me.
I feel that if I have to move,
When my last day is here,
I think that I'll find Heaven
No lovelier, or more loving than
My daffodils and family care.

Daffodil morning

Golden, girded garden
Lit by early sun.
Birds on the grass feeding,
Pecking one by one.

Blue tits on the nut frame,
Bright in mating hue
Waiting on the clothes line
In patient, orderly queue.

Each mother a Mary,
Each son a Christ,
They died that we might live.
Some fought because they had to,
Some fought because they must.
But when the stone is rolled away,
The stone we now call 'Death',
We shall be told as Mary was told
Where we may meet again.
Mothers of sons who died too young,
Wives whose husbands were lost,
Will meet again their loved ones
Who did not count the cost.

I walked alone beneath the stars
To leave the world behind,
To free myself from prison bars,
A family good and kind.

Too much pressed down as youth became
Manhood, that age of fears.
How to escape from ties and deign
To stifle back the tears.

I am a son, a brother too,
A neighbour, friend and foe.
How can I shake my own self free,
Do what I needs must do?

The stars were far, the silence full,
I stood and felt alone.
T'was then I knew, and thus know still:
I am myself. I am my own.

I knew a man, who knew a man,
Who had an Uncle Jack
Went out to sea in a fishing boat
And brought a mermaid back.

I did not see her for myself,
Nor did the man I knew,
But the man who had an Uncle Jack
Said her hair was blue.

I knew a man, who knew a man,
Who had an Uncle Jack
Went out to sea in a fishing boat
And threw the mermaid back...
SPLASH!!!

A Shropshire lad,
They said,
Would be strong I' th' arm,
And thick i' the 'ead.
But bending over this tiny cot,
All I can see is a smile and a tot.
A bundle of softness,
A baby so lovely,
So gurgly and happy,
Carelessly dribbling
The last of his feed.
Newborn beauty,
Smiling at me,
Making me happy,
As happy can be.
When you've grown old, you forget
That miracles happen.
Misty my eyes, but not through years,
Misty my eyes with grateful tears.
Hopes for the future, when arms will mature
And a mind will grow agile ... in Shropshire air.

Elizabeth, Elizabeth,
Lillybet my own.
Eyes so bright
And hair so soft,
Soft as thistledown.

Fingers long
To grip and say,
'All my love to you this day.'

You it was that brought me here,
You it is I'll hold most dear.
In your arms in peace and calm,
Safe with you, I'll take no harm.

When you are old
You can't jump for joy,
As when you're a boy
And can jump to touch a leaf
Or almost the sky.

When you are old
You can still have the joy.
No need to jump,
Joy jumps to meet you.

Just look through the window,
See the hills in the sun,
Feel the glory of springtime
Just bursting through.

Hear the baby shouting with glee,
Blue-eyed, rosy-cheeked, as happy can be.
He like the old cannot jump, it's true,
But the joy is all there, just bursting through.

Part Three

My Poems for My Father

Let there be time to sigh
When I look into your eyes
And think of the times we have had.

Let there be time to cry
When you shall die,
For I shall lose my lifelong friend.

Let there be time to smile
When I pause awhile
To explain to the children what's happened.

And let there be time to muse
Whenever I choose
To think and talk of you.

How often it is I wish you were here,
How often it causes a silent tear.
Why can't you watch us, listen and smile?
Couldn't you come and stay just for a while?

We've so much to give you, so much to share.
Why is it, Grandad, you can't be there?
We can count and write and almost read too.
Why is it, Grandad, we can't show you?

There is no one to share with,
No one who knows.
I never really realised
That our world was so enclosed.

It makes our love more precious,
But parting worse to bear.
No one seems to understand
My hurt that you're not there.

I wake with you beside me,
Within me and without,
But I know that you are nowhere –
Your death leaves me no doubt.

In influence and genes
I guess you always will live on,
But any life in any form
I am quite sure has gone.

I love you more than words can say
And wish that you were here
But cruel death has stolen you
Clean away.

The first year that my Dad was not here for Christmas

So, Christmas went quite well this year.
Mince pies, wine and seasonal cheer,
Family visits and presents galore.
Still I wish that you could have been here.

I managed the carols and the Christmas story,
The wise men, shepherds and the Angels' glory
Without a flinch or trace of care.
Just maybe here and there a tear.

You shared your wisdom, gave me strength,
When we had time, we'd talk at length.
Why was it then you had to go?
Why is it I still miss you so?

Early spring

Somewhere under the bracken
My daffodils will be shooting,
Bulbs I planted in the rain
The January day we spread your ashes.

I try to shelter beneath a tree,
But winter has stolen the leaves
And large drops land heavily on my head.
It's better to weather the fine drizzle in the open.

And just think on...

How well the oaks have grown around you,
Ash have sprouted too.
'Natural regeneration' they do say,
But I think it's you!

So much for recycling.
But my love can never change,
You are my constant believer,
For ever and for always by my side.

Can a year have drifted by
Without you being here?
Without my snuggling close to you
And you whispering in my ear?

A year without your letters
And the chocolate parcels too,
A year without my weekly dose
Of the essence of you.

Life goes on as you said it would,
But oh I miss you so.
Souls like yours should linger long –
Why did you have to go?

So many things for you to see,
So much to make you smile,
Talks we always meant to have
If life could have paused awhile.

Memories and new landmarks
I wish I could share with you.
But death offers no compromise:
There's nothing I can do.

And so our lives continue,
Happy and well blessed.
Is it selfish still to love you
And not let your memory rest?

But you are part of me and them,
Why should we not feel riven?
Your soul will never die with us,
Us your begotten children.

Part Four

My Poems for My Children

My father said that you should give your children two
things: roots and wings.

This is a small collection of poems written during the time
that our children were spreading their wings and I was
coming to terms with a different parental role.

For Our Children

These are the times I will treasure,
Memories I will hold locked tight
In my heart for ever.

You make me smile and laugh and sing,
I love to be with you and share everything,
But I know I must let you go.

So thanks for the nights and days of care
The smiles and swims and just being there.
Away you fly, I love you.

How can I ever explain how much I love you?
As far as the wind can reach or the sun can see.
How will you ever know the value of your friendship,
Your smiles and hugs and loving looks?

How can you ever know how much you mean to me?
More than the stars can sparkle or the moon can
shine.
How will you ever know the joy you have brought
By being you and loving me?

I keep trying to find a moment
To say some things to you,
To thank you for your care
And all the thoughtful things you do.

You are so kind and helpful,
The very best of pals,
Always watching, always hugging
When you know I need a boost.

My love for you is really more
Than simple words can say,
So I've picked some special flowers
And pressed them for a day ... or two...

Heartsease and a daffodil
From very special places,
They are for you because you are
The very best of daughters!

I wish that I could say
All the wise things he'd have said,
To keep you safe and happy
On the road that lies ahead.

I wish that he was here to smile
And take you in his arms,
To wink and raise a glass to you.
He'd be so very proud.

But anyway, it's just me here,
Trying to write a rhyme
To match the cool 'arrival pome'
He wrote when you were born.

And as before there are coins to keep
To mark your special year.
Keep them for ever and always be sure of
The unflinching love they hold whatever,
whenever,
wherever you are.

It's so hard, so hard...
Every day I've seen you,
Every day we've talked,
Every day we've come to terms
With the world.

Now you've gone,
You're independent,
You can choose, enjoy and fly,
Make judgements and go your own way.

I just have to trust in our history.
Have I said the right thing enough times?
I know you will you make the right choices,
And see through false promises.

I trust in your judgement,
Your strength and determination,
And send you love by various means,
And know that you will succeed, but I miss you.
XXX

There is a thread between our hearts,
I feel it anyway.
I hope it helps a little bit
To ease the pain away.

It always will just be there,
Invisible and strong.
Nothing will ever break it,
You will never be alone.

I love you in the morning,
And I love you when it's night,
I love you when it's raining
Or the sun is shining bright!

I love you when you're happy,
And I love you when you're sad,
I love you when you're worried
Or you're very, very glad!

I love you when you're working,
And I love you when you play.
I love you when you're winning
Or you've had a long hard day!

I love you when you're near me
And I love you far away,
I love you so much all the time,
More and more each day!

My love for you will never end,
However life pans out.
My love is always here for you,
You never need to doubt.

Tonight my son lies in his bed,
So I may safely rest my head
On my pillow in contentment.

I know he's close, I know he's safe,
I can peak in and see his face
Sleeping softly on his pillow.

He has to go, he has to stand
Alone and forge his way, I know.
But how I love it when he's home!

Hey, it's late, near midnight,
But I can hear your voice
On-line talking to someone.
Whoever, you are close.

It's been so very lovely
To have you home awhile.
I can pop and see you any time,
Soak up your awesome smile.

I know you have to go again,
I know that it is right.
I just can't help but miss you
When you're gone and out of sight.

I cling to things and memories,
But you're always pretty near.
You may be many miles away,
But you are always in my heart.

I think of you when I go to sleep
And I think of you when I wake.
I love it when I hear from you,
I smile to know you're safe.

Perhaps I should just let you go –
I am confident you'd survive!
But it's just so lovely to keep in touch,
And hear about your new lives

Thank you.

It's hard when we are lambing,
It happens every year,
I get busy, tired and anxious
And often shed a tear.

But this year it is better,
You are there to hug and smile,
Just round every corner,
Bringing calm for just a while.

I catch your eye from time to time,
You understand my pain.
You're there to share the good bits,
The sunshine and the rain.

So thanks for all your hard work,
And just for being there.
You've helped me through the hard time
With all your love and care.

Well, that's what you do...
You bring them up to be capable,
Independent, hard-working and strong,
And then you find they can get along
Without you!

The odd cash is always handy,
And care parcels always fine,
But in their busy schedules
There actually isn't much time.

Which of course is as it should be.
I'm as proud as proud can be,
Of two children coping magnificently –
Without me!

But, I'm always thinking about them,
I can't seem to quite let go.
So if, just if, anyone needs me,
I'll always be here, you know.

The first night you're away,
Maybe that is the worst.
You might be here, but you're not.

I see your face so clear,
You seem so very near,
But you're not here.
I know.

But I can picture you
In another room,
Another place, maybe...

Does it matter where you are?
Close to home or very far?
For you're always you and I'm always me,
There for each other for all eternity.

The summer has flown
And time moved on.
I cannot believe you will be gone
And I will be here without you.

So much to achieve, so much to do,
But so much of the time I'm thinking of you!
I wish you all you wish yourself,
In studies, life and everything else!

I'll look in your room –
You won't be there,
But I'll treasure the memories
Of when you were.

But still...

I'll be waiting to hear your news
And talk to you now and again.
You'll not be far, never far away
From my loving you, night and day –
24/7 as they say...

Always here for you.

Will I ever get used to it?
I don't think so...
You are part of my life, my body, my soul,
Without you I don't feel whole.

But I'll love you whatever, wherever you are,
If you're in the same room or away very far.
I'll always be here if you need me at all,
Just send me a text or give me a call.
I'm so proud of all that you are and do,
And so happy to be a mum for you!

Last night I waited,
This morning I watched,
I knew you were coming.
You slept so sound.

But you were close,
You were near.
Today you were here
To smile at,
To hold,
To listen to,
And be so proud.
Just for a while
You were here,
And I smiled,
It was so good.

What a day it's been...
We set off, both of us, full of dreams.
But the reality was painful and hard.

How did we make it back to the car,
So far?
And then the long journey home...

I wished I could fly
You through the sky,
Back home to safety.

You stood it,
You prevailed,
You never once complained.
But beside you I felt so helpless.
I so wanted to whisk you home,
To safety, to calm,
To comfort and arms to love you.

We made it, you slept,
Waking later tired but beautiful.

Why didn't they tell us?
Why didn't they say
It was going to be such a difficult day?

Caramel Waffles

Today we went to Starbucks,
And we thought so much of you
We bought a little something
We thought would see you through
Any little pangs of hunger
You might feel throughout the day.
Well, we thought you would enjoy them anyway!

Part Five

My Poems

Blue haze under Mordran,
A sort of forget-me-not blue.
My mind dwells on days gone by,
Unforgotten, unforgettable times.

The blue of the sea where we learned to swim,
The sky where we flew the kite so high,
The carpet we played on and sat on and walked on,
The Rover that fetched us and carried.

I gaze at the blueness and I try to capture
The meaning of life and love.
But my transient grasp of significance
Fades with the blueness.

Down through the wood piece,
Wind whistling through my hair,
The bronze yellow sunlight
Playing on the air.

The green, the gold, the purple,
Visual images overwhelmed
Quite suddenly by a deeply
Pungent, all-embracing smell.

It was the smell of autumn.
Suddenly I knew,
Everything within me
Was encompassed in that hue.

The sight is to be wondered,
But to live the very feel
Of autumn in one's soul
Is more than mortals dare reveal.

Homeward, weary, wends the farmer
With his trailer laden down.
Straw a-plenty for the winter,
Bedding for the sheep and cows.

The sun has shone, the rain's held off
The combine's come and gone,
Taking the grain and leaving the swath
For balers yet to come.

When the winter winds blow hardest
And the blizzard closes in,
Calves can snuggle next to Mother,
Bedded in the building.

Ewes grown heavy, late with twins,
Nuzzle in the straw.
Some cleave with foot amongst the strands
To make a nest upon the floor.

So, for grain, you barons keep it,
We have all the gold,
Straw to bed the beasts and keep them
Safe within our fold.

My father tells a story
Of his springtime show of glory,
A time when beauty will array
Our garden with a fine display.

Each year in a stupendous row,
Though bulbs or such we never sow,
A great wide patch of yellow breaks
As once again the trumpet wakes.

Amid a sea of leafy green
A better show was never seen,
Proud, erect and tall they stand
A golden carpet on our land.

Our farewell to you
Is a day I will treasure.
Emotions at peak
And tensions so high,
All locked in our own private memories,
Each facing the day in our own way.

I cannot believe how you wrote and spoke
Of the memories close to our hearts.
Thank you for sharing and putting into words
That which I could not.

You came and were such a support to us all,
I'll never forget you squeezing my hand
And I smile to remember the journey home,
You on your most amusing form,
Lifting and drifting the sadness.

And thank you for being by my side,
Constant but not intrusive,
Keeping everyone in conversation,
Allowing me the space I needed.

No more visits, no more games,
No more chocolate or birthday parties,
But a plethora of thoughts and memories
And a place amongst us for ever.

They rise from the loch,
Acute and straight,
And with ancient patience
They sit and wait.

Sometimes their peaks
Are lost in mist
As their tears flow quietly
For life's loves missed.

Hands joined for ever
Under the changing sky,
The sisters remain
As time goes by.

To my faithful hound

I often feel a sense of guilt
As I look into your soft brown eyes
When you snuggle up against the quilt
And stretch your arm to mine.

You were my first-loved baby,
It was you I fed and spoiled,
But then came changes and maybe
Both our worlds were in turmoil.

New 'animals' within the fold
Claiming first attention,
Leaving you out in the cold,
Not understanding the tension.

Perhaps only now I turn to you,
Now my babies can cope alone.
You're waiting there, a friend that's true,
Smiling back at me.

We used to pick sloes,
We used to plant trees,
And sometimes round up sheep.
There were cattle to feed
And bonfires to have,
There was wind to blow cobwebs away.

Everything's here,
Little has changed,
'Jobs' still need to be done,
But you're not here,
And you don't know
How my life meanders on.

You used to phone when you were going
And say 'Hi' when you got back,
We used to touch each other's bases
And there was comfort in that.

You used to feed the cattle,
Slit the plastic, cut the string.
We used to smell of silage, cows,
And other 'farmy' things.

You used to come and walk alone
Amongst the bells and hills.
I wondered if you'd settle near
To your 'heart an air that kills'.

But you've moved on, your life has changed,
And for you I must be glad.
You've time to share and time to spare,
Why should I then be sad?

Our time will come again, daresay,
One of these autumn days
The sun will shine through falling leaves
And gone will be the rain.

If you are looking
You will find me.
If you need me
I'll be there.
If you want to chat
Just call me.
If it's hard
I want to share your pain.

For trouble shared
Is halved, they say,
And every day is another day
To live and enjoy life's journey,
Smooth or rough along the track,
Looking forwards more than back,
Taking one day at a time together.